FRIDA KAHLO

Mexican Painter

Kristen Woronoff

BLACKBIRCH PRESS

THOMSON

GALE

Detroit • New York • San Diego • San Francisco
Boston • New Haven, Conn. • Waterville, Maine
London • Munich

Published by Blackbirch Press
10911 Technology Place
San Diego, CA 92127
e-mail: customerservice@galegroup.com
Web site: http://www.galegroup.com/blackbirch

Printed in China

10 9 8 7 6 5 4 3 2 1

Photo credits:
Cover, page 20 © Delores Olmedo; cover inset © International Museum of Photography at George Eastman House; pages 3, 9, 16, 19, 23, 24 © CORBIS, pages 4, 6 © Mexican Government Tourist Office; pages 8, 13 © Guillermo Kahlo; page 11 © ENP-UNAM; pages 14, 31 © I.N.B.A. Munal; page 17 © AP/Wide World Photos, page 18 © The Library of Congress; page 27 © Schalkwijk/Art Resource, NY; page 28 © Frida Kahlo Museum, Mexico

Library of Congress Cataloging-in-Publication Data
Woronoff, Kristen.
Frida Kahlo / by Kristen Woronoff.
        p. cm. — (Famous women juniors)
Summary: Introduces the life of the world-famous Mexican artist who overcame polio, injuries from a near-fatal bus accident, a tempestuous marriage to Diego Rivera, and other difficulties.
        ISBN 1-56711-594-2
1. Kahlo, Frida—Juvenile literature. 2. Painters—Mexico—Biography—Juvenile literature. [1. Kahlo, Frida. 2. Artists. 3. Women-Biography.] I. Title. II. Series.
ND259.K33 W67 2002
759.972—dc21   2001005131

Frida Kahlo was a painter. Many people say that she was one of Mexico's greatest artists. Yet few people today know the story of this unusual woman who overcame personal problems and disabilities to create colorful paintings and murals.

Early Life

The small town of Coyoacán, Mexico, is about an hour from Mexico City, the country's capital. On a street corner in Coyoacán is a bright blue house. This is the house in which Frida Kahlo was born on July 6, 1907.

Frida's father was Wilhelm Kahlo. He grew up in Germany. When he was 19, Wilhelm Kahlo left Germany and never returned. He settled in Mexico and changed his name to Guillermo Kahlo. Guillermo was a photographer who enjoyed painting as a hobby.

Frida Kahlo was born in a town near Mexico City (pictured).

Guillermo married a Mexican woman. They had two children. Then, his wife died. After his first wife's death, Guillermo married Frida's mother, Matilde. Guillermo's oldest children did not live with the new family. Instead, they were sent away, and did not visit often.

The Kahlos had two children before Frida. They had one more daughter after Frida was born.

When Frida was six years old, she became very sick. She had terrible pains in her legs. Doctors discovered she had polio, a disease that damages the nervous system.

Frida Kahlo's work was influenced by ancient Mexican art.

It took Frida nine months to recover from the illness. During that time, she spent many long hours alone in her own make-believe world. She pretended to enter the world by fogging a window with her breath. She would then draw a door on the fogged window. Her imagination would take her through that door. In her make-believe world, she had a friend who was a happy child. The make-believe friend listened to Frida's problems and cheered her up.

The illness left one of Frida's legs weak and thinner than the other. To help her leg become stronger, Frida's father made sure she played sports, such as soccer, boxing, wrestling, and swimming. Frida also liked to climb trees and play ball, which were unusual activities for girls at that time.

Frida's father often shared art books with her. Sometimes she watched while he painted. He showed her how to use a camera. He also taught her how to color photographs by hand to make them more pleasing to the eye.

Despite her health problems, Frida grew up as a fun-loving child who was often full of mischief.

Meeting a Famous Artist

In 1922, when she was 15, Frida went to the best high school in Mexico, the National Preparatory School in Mexico City. Only 35 of the 2,000 students there were girls. There were both rich and poor students there. Frida made many new friends in school. She also became a member of a group called the Cachuchas. They were known for their intelligence and for their mischief.

Frida attended high school in Mexico City.

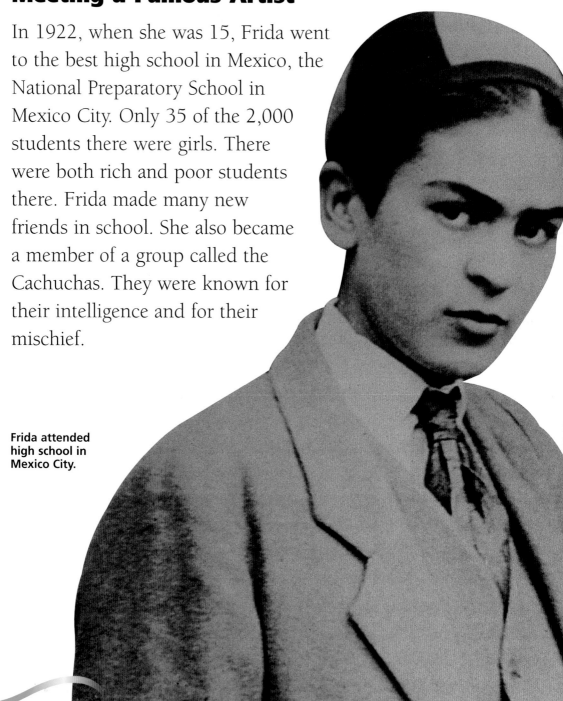

8

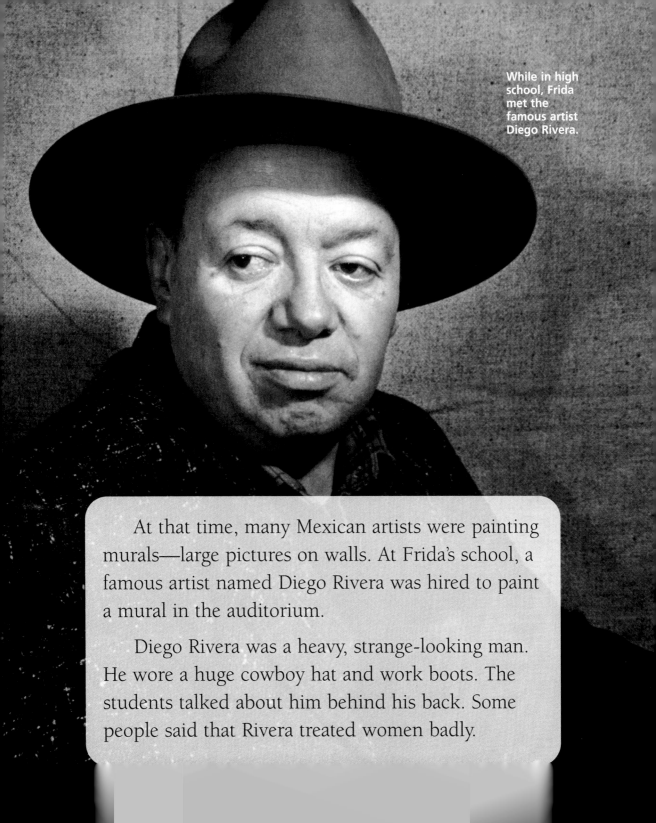

At that time, many Mexican artists were painting murals—large pictures on walls. At Frida's school, a famous artist named Diego Rivera was hired to paint a mural in the auditorium.

Diego Rivera was a heavy, strange-looking man. He wore a huge cowboy hat and work boots. The students talked about him behind his back. Some people said that Rivera treated women badly.

The wall Rivera planned to paint was the huge back wall of the stage. He decided to paint a story from the Bible. The people he painted were larger than life. They were all painted in bright colors. He also painted both light- and dark-skinned people to show the different races of people in Mexico.

The students at the school were not allowed in the auditorium while Rivera was painting. But Frida would sneak in and watch him working high on a ladder. Sometimes she called up to him in a teasing voice. She took food out of his lunch basket and played other tricks on him. To other girls, it seemed like Frida had a crush on the strange-looking artist.

It took Rivera a year to finish the mural. And when he finished, many people thought it was ugly. The mural created a lot of questions about art.

Frida liked the mural, but she did not have strong feelings for Rivera. Instead, she loved a young man a few years ahead of her in school named Alejandro Gómez Arias. He was the leader of the Cachuchas. The two often spent time together after school. When they were apart, they wrote letters to each other. Frida decorated her letters with funny drawings.

Young women were not supposed to go on dates alone with young men in those days in Mexico. Frida had to make up excuses to meet Alejandro. For two years, Frida and Alejandro saw each other as often as possible.

Frida met Diego Rivera whle he was working on this mural, titled *Creation*.

A Terrible Accident

After finishing school, the young couple decided to take a trip to the United States together. Frida wanted to save money for a trip, but she had to give her money to her family. She worked as a cashier, a factory worker, and even a printer's helper.

On September 17, 1925, Frida and Alejandro were sitting in the back of a crowded bus. Suddenly, a trolley, a train that ran on city streets, crashed into the bus. The force of the trolley broke the bus into pieces. As the trolley kept moving, it crushed people who fell beneath it and people inside the bus.

Frida was seriously injured. A piece of railing went through her body. "A handrail pierced me the way a sword pierces a bull," she wrote years later. Her spine was broken in three places. Her collarbone and her ribs were broken. Her right leg was broken in 11 places. Her foot was twisted and crushed. Her shoulder was twisted out of place. Her pelvis was broken in three places.

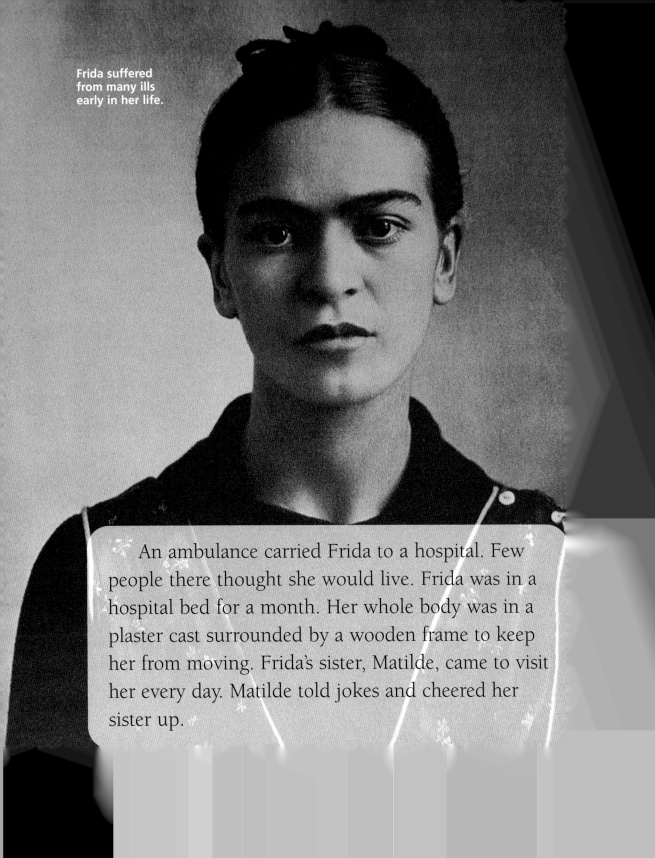

Frida suffered from many ills early in her life.

An ambulance carried Frida to a hospital. Few people there thought she would live. Frida was in a hospital bed for a month. Her whole body was in a plaster cast surrounded by a wooden frame to keep her from moving. Frida's sister, Matilde, came to visit her every day. Matilde told jokes and cheered her sister up.

Frida painted this self-portrait in the early 1920s.

Alejandro was also hurt in the accident. He stayed home to recover. Frida wrote him many letters. Frida went home one month after the accident.

While she was recovering at home, Frida had to sit still all the time. To keep busy, she began to paint. She began by painting pictures of her friends. During the summer of 1926, she started her first self-portrait. The self-portrait was a gift for Alejandro. She hoped it would bring him back to her. But she was wrong. He had decided to travel to Europe without her. When he returned home, things between them had changed forever.

Meeting Rivera Again

As Frida recovered, she made a new group of friends. Her new friends were followers of communism, a political system that did not support the ownership of private property. Diego Rivera was a member of the Communist Party. The two met again at the Mexican Ministry of Public Education, where Diego was painting a second mural.

Diego Rivera was painting another mural when he and Frida met for the second time.

Just as he had before, Diego stood on a ladder to paint. Frida called up to him. But this time, it was not to tease. She had some of her paintings for him to see. "Diego, come down," she said. She wanted to know what he thought of her work.

Later, Diego said that was one of the happiest days of his life. He liked Frida's dark hair and eyebrows. They started spending a great deal of time together. Frida was happy, and she painted more. Soon, the strange-looking man and the injured young woman began to talk about marriage.

Frida and Diego lived in this house in Mexico City when they were first married.

Frida and Diego posed for this picture in 1932.

Finally, they were married, and moved into a house in Mexico City. Because he owned property and was becoming wealthy from his work, Diego was asked to leave the Communist Party. He left, but always remained a communist at heart.

Soon after their marriage, Frida told her husband that she wanted to visit the United States. In 1930, the couple moved to California. In California, Frida painted a wedding picture of herself and Diego. The painting shows how different they were. Diego was more than 6 feet tall and weighed 300 pounds. Frida was 5 feet 3 inches and weighed less than 100 pounds.

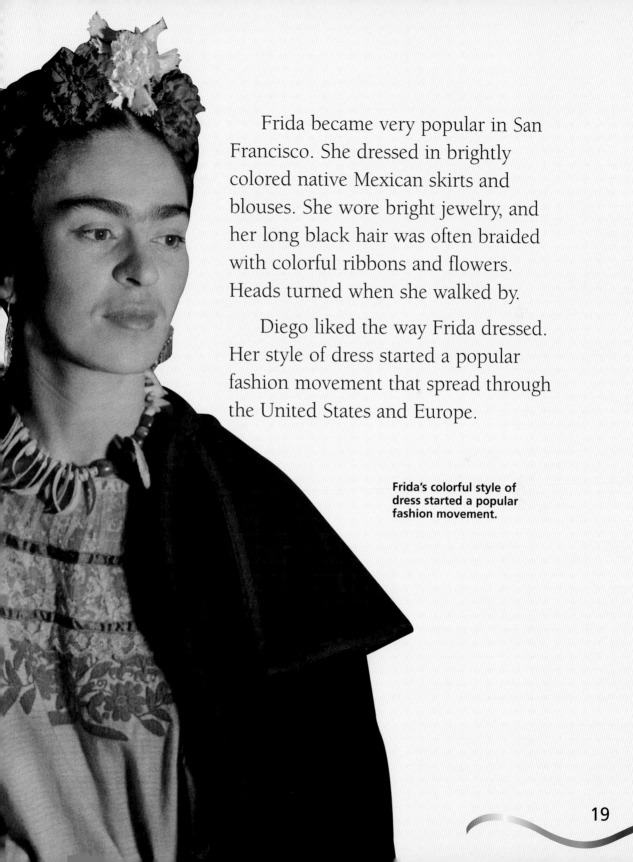

Frida became very popular in San Francisco. She dressed in brightly colored native Mexican skirts and blouses. She wore bright jewelry, and her long black hair was often braided with colorful ribbons and flowers. Heads turned when she walked by.

Diego liked the way Frida dressed. Her style of dress started a popular fashion movement that spread through the United States and Europe.

Frida's colorful style of dress started a popular fashion movement.

Frida painted this portrait of the plant scientist Luther Burbank.

Married Life

Diego focused on painting while Frida explored the city and its museums on her own. She became friends with a surgeon, Dr. Leo Eloesser. She painted his picture and gave it to him as a gift. She also painted the famous plant scientist Luther Burbank.

Finally, Frida decided that she did not enjoy living in San Francisco as much as she thought she would. She and Diego returned to Mexico in 1931 and started to build a house there. Shortly afterward, however, Diego was asked to show his paintings at the Museum of Modern Art in New York City. The couple moved to New York in November 1931.

After a short stay in New York City, Diego was asked to paint murals in Detroit, Michigan, where most of the country's cars were being built. Frida and Diego moved to Detroit. While living there, Frida produced some of her best and most famous artwork.

By that time, Frida's mother had become ill. Frida began to paint in a new style that expressed her sadness. All of Frida's artwork was very personal. It helped Frida deal with the sadness and tragedy in her life.

When Diego finished his work in Detroit, he was asked to paint a mural in Rockefeller Center in New York City. The mural caused many arguments. People thought Diego was painting his political beliefs about communism. By that time, many people felt that communism was a dangerous political belief. Diego was asked to stop work, even though the mural was not finished. He was paid for his work, but the mural was destroyed.

Diego Rivera at work on a mural.

Diego always supported Frida as a painter.

As the months in the United States passed, Diego and Frida began to fight more often. Frida was still in terrible pain from her accident many years earlier. She created a painting called *My Dress Hangs There*, which represented a feeling that she wanted to return home to Mexico for good.

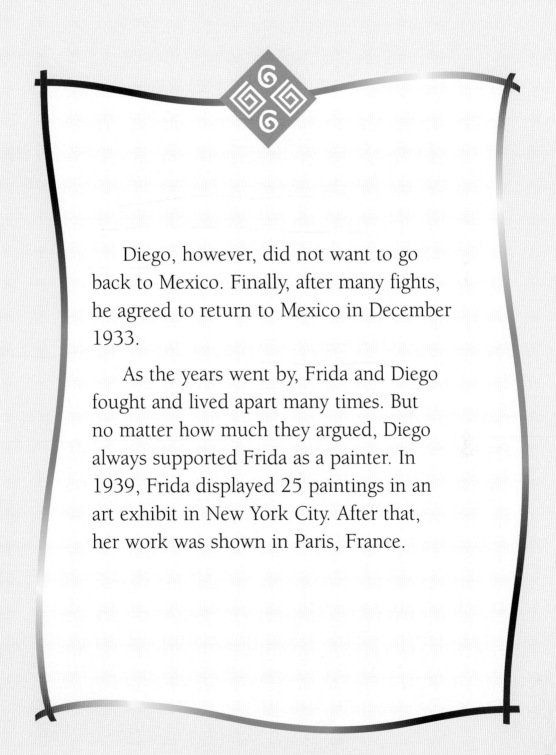

Diego, however, did not want to go back to Mexico. Finally, after many fights, he agreed to return to Mexico in December 1933.

As the years went by, Frida and Diego fought and lived apart many times. But no matter how much they argued, Diego always supported Frida as a painter. In 1939, Frida displayed 25 paintings in an art exhibit in New York City. After that, her work was shown in Paris, France.

Painted Monkeys

Some of Frida's most famous paintings were self-portraits. In many of these paintings, Frida placed one or more monkeys in the background. Frida had monkeys as pets. She also had many other pets: parrots, deer, dogs, and even an eagle. But few of these animals appear in her paintings.

Many people think Frida used the monkeys in her paintings to express some important feelings that she had. No one knows for sure. Some people think she kept monkeys as pets because she did not have any children. Frida may have put monkeys in her paintings as a way to show that she wished for children.

Frida painted this *Self-portrait with Monkey* in 1945.

Frida included a small picture of Diego in this self-portrait.

By the early 1950s, the damage to Frida's body from the accident many years earlier grew worse. She spent a whole year in the hospital. Her leg had to be removed. But through it all, she continued to paint.

In 1953, her paintings were shown in Mexico. An ambulance drove Frida to the exhibit. She enjoyed the party lying on a stretcher. The next year, in 1954, Frida Kahlo died at age 47.

Diego Rivera was deeply saddened by Frida's death. He said that when she died, he realized how much he loved her. And he knew that her artwork was always great. He said that she had always been a better painter than he was.

Frida Kahlo's work did not become very popular until 30 years after her death. Today, she is considered to be one of the world's greatest painters.

The blue house in Coyoacán where Frida Kahlo was born is now a museum. Thousands of people visit it every year. Though she is gone, Frida's spirit still seems to live there in her colorful, unusual paintings.

The Two Fridas is another of Frida's self-portraits.

Glossary

Artist A person who creates something by using imagination and creative skill.

Communism A political system that does not support the ownership of private property.

Hobby A leisure-time activity.

Mischief Irresponsibly playful.

Mural A work of art, usually a painting, on a wall.

Portrait A picture representing a person, usually showing the person's face.

Unusual Out of the ordinary.

For More Information

Websites

Frida Kahlo and Contemporary Thoughts
www.fridakahlo.it

Website includes a brief biography, contemporary essays, a short movie about Kahlo, and a large bibliography.

The World of Frida Kahlo
http://members.aol.com/fridanet/kahlo.htm

This comprehensive website offers a biography, quotes from Kahlo, Kahlo's paintings, facts, and links to other sites.

Books

Boris, Janet. *Frida Kahlo (Art Ed Kits)*. New York: Harry N. Abrams, 2001.

Garza, Hedda and Green, Robert. *Frida Kahlo (Hispanics of Achievement)*. Broomall, PA: Chelsea House, 2002.

Venezia, Mike. *Frida Kahlo (Getting to Know the World's Greatest Artists)*. Danbury, CT: Children's Press, 1999.

Index

Burbank, Luther, 21

Cachuchas, 8, 11
Communism, 16, 18, 22
Coyoacán 4, 30

Eloesser, Dr. Leo, 21

Fashion movement, 19

Gómez, Alejandro, 11, 12, 15

Kahlo, Frida,
  Father, Wilhelm-Guillermo, 4-5, 7

Make-believe world of, 6
Marriage to Diego Rivera, 18
Mother, Matilde, 5, 22
Polio, 5-7
Self-portraits, 15, 26
Sister, Matilde, 13

My Dress Hangs There, 24
Museum of Modern Art, 21

National Preparatory School, 8

Monkeys, 26

Rivera, Diego, 9-11, 16-19, 21-22, 25-29